Dear Parents,

Matty's Heart, A Child and Parents Guide To Open Heart Surgery, was written about Matthew Lewis's experience. Though we attempted to keep it general, it does tell Matthews story. Please check with your doctor or nurse educator on how things will differ for your child.

I suggest you read the book for yourself first, so you can better understand yourself before starting to prepare your child. This book has been written at an approximate 8 year old level in the child's section. Please see the chart below on one suggested way to gear this to the understanding level of your child. You know your child best, use your instinct in editing the material for their best understanding. We normally start preparing Matt a few days in advance for his hospitalizations. This gives him a chance to talk about his fears and prepare emotionally. Page 22 and 23 discuss Matt fear of dying. You may want to review ahead of time, and edit in accordance to your beliefs and your own child's fears. Again you are the parent and **YOU** know your child best.

Please feel free to write me with your experience with the use of this book.

Sincerely yours,

Jean Clabough RN

UNDERSTANDING LEVEL CHART
(Highlight what you want to read to our child with a highlighter)

12 mo - 3 yr	Just look at the pictures and Mr Pump. Can say short phrases like "Orange Soap that's silly" Pg 24 & Pg 25, or "Peek-a-boo I see you" Pg 14 & 15.
4 yrs - 6 yrs	Can probably understand approximately 3 sentences per page. Example Pg 26 & 27 read lines 1 - 4 and last line. Then if they ask other questions, just answer them.
7 yrs - 10 yrs	Read large print. If they ask questions you can't answer be sure you write them down to ask the doctor or nurse.
11 yrs & up	Let them read it themselves. Be sure to discuss it with your child and encourage them to write down any questions they may have.

MATTY'S HEART

A Child's and Parents Guide to
Open Heart Surgery

Jean Clabough, R.N.

Illustrations By Sandra Sovern-Leedham

Technical advisor: M.W. Cocalis M.D.
Pediatric Cardiologist

**CHILD'S AND PARENTS'
MEDICAL STORYBOOKS
VOLUME I**

ALETHEIA PUBLISHING

San Bernardino, California 92408

Matty's Heart

Copyright © 1995
Elgene Leah Clabough RN

All rights reserved. No part of this publication may be reproduced, stored in a retrievable system, or transmitted in any form or by any means except for brief quotations in printed reviews without the prior permission of the Author or Publisher. For more information write
Aletheia Publishing, 1814 Commercenter West, Suite G, San Bernardino, CA 92408

Publisher's Cataloging-in-Publication Data

Clabough, Jean, 1947
    Matty's Heart, A Child's and Parents Guide to Open Heart Surgery
        Child's and Parents Medical Storybooks Vol. I
    Elgene Leah Clabough
        p. cm.
    1. Open heart surgery - Juvenile literature 1. Title
J617.412   1995   CIP 94-071677 1995
ISBN 09638662-3-0

Illustrations by Sandra Sovern-Leedham

Technical Advise by M.W. Cocalis M.D

Proofreading by Debbie Polk

Printed in Hong Kong

Published By Aletheia Publishing
1814 Commercenter West, Suite G
San Bernardino, CA 92408

DEDICATED TO
My grandson, Matthew David Lewis, who underwent this surgery four times, inspiring me to write this book. My parents, Col. Elgin L. Hushbeck Sr. and Gertrude G. Hushbeck

With special thanks to: M.W. Cocalis M.D., for his dedication and expertise in caring for my grandson. Hannelore & Elgin Hushbeck Jr., for their support, advice and encouragement, and Pastor Dennis & Debbie Polk for their prayers and love.

This book belongs to

_____

Date of surgery

_____

Type of surgery done

_____

_____

Doctors names

_____ _____

_____ _____

INTRODUCTION

While working at a children's hospital as a pediatric nurse, I was given a preop child who was going to have open heart surgery the next morning. He was 9 years old, his parents were not with him and he was scared. My only tools were a scrap book that had no information on what to expect and a tour of the ICU. The ICU nurse showed him a fresh open heart surgery patient. While there, the surgery patient started coughing and sputtering and needed suctioning. The 9 year old was more terrified after seeing this, than if he had not had preop teaching at all. This came back to haunt me as my grandson faced 3 more open heart surgeries (total of 4) and I myself went through a similiar type of surgery. My grandson had his surgeries as an infant, but possibly faces more throughout his life. I want him to be prepared, but in a less threatening way. It wasn't until my own surgery that I fully understood the emotions and pain involved in this type of surgery. As an adult, I knew the recovery period was temporary. Knowing what to expect helped me to tolerate the ET tube, Chest tubes, the pain, being unable to communicate (talk), the noise (respirators, monitors, beeping), and worst of all the suctioning. I knew it was temporary! A child goes to sleep, possibly in his mother's arms, and awakes to find he's tied down, can't make a sound, and is in tremendous pain, which makes him terrified. He doesn't understand that this is a temporary situation and begins fighting everything. Naturally this causes additional strain on him and additional use of medication which can prolong his recovery.

This book is designed to help prepare both the child and parents or guardians, for this necessary surgery that so many of them face. Since open heart surgery is a very complex procedure, with the care varying from doctor to doctor and hospital to hospital, I have attempted to make this book as generic as possible. Only the basics will be covered. Children's ages and understanding vary considerably, so the book is written in 2 parts: the first part with Mr. Pump for younger children, the boxed part for older children, parents & guardians. You, as the parent, can modify either part to the best understanding level of your child.

Disclaimer: 1. All medical staff and children or adults in this story except for the immediate family are fictional. If any resemblance occurs, it is purely accidental. 2. Matthew actually had the surgery described when he was 7 months old. Many scenes in the pictures were taken from pictures taken during his many angioplasties, with the appropriate equipment added.

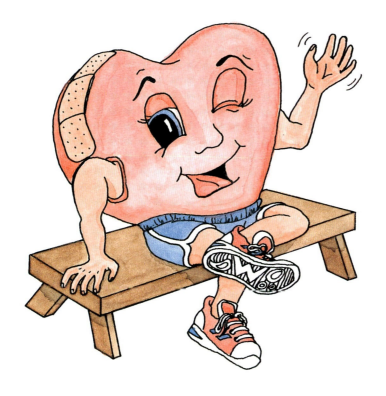

Hi! My name is Mr. Pump. I'm a heart. A heart pumps your blood all over your body. I want to tell you a story about a 4 year old boy named Matty. His heart doesn't work right. Matty didn't do anything wrong to make his heart not work right. His Mommy and Daddy didn't do anything wrong either. It is just how he was born. Matty is a very brave and special little boy.

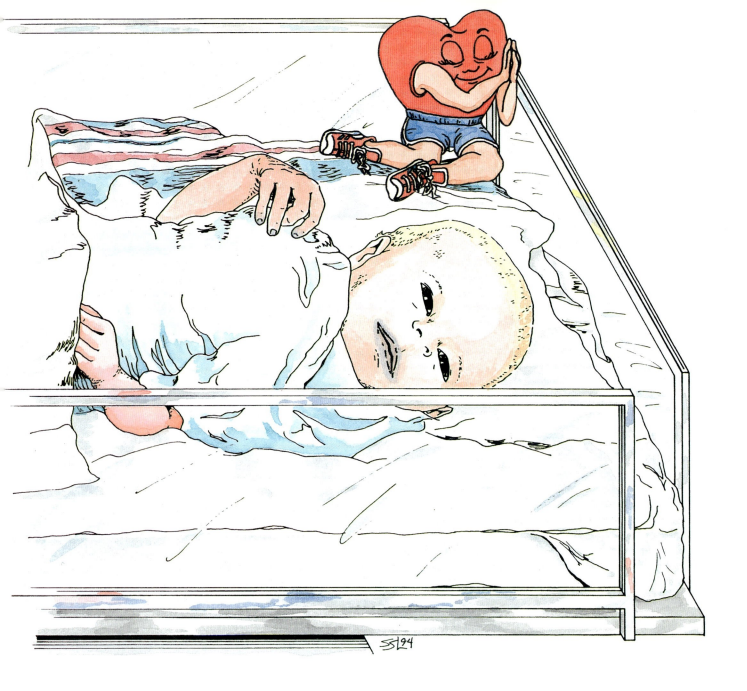

This is Matty when he was born. See the blue around his lips? The blue is because his heart is broken. The doctors fixed his heart when he was 10 days old. He see's his doctor every year to have his heart checked.

Cardiac problems are not always apparent at birth, sometimes it can be hours, days, months, or even years before a problem is found. For instance, the heart problem of the 9 year old mentioned in the introduction was not found until he was 9. My grandson's was not found until a few hours after birth, as his body switched from fetal circulation to his own circulation. If he had also been born with a hole in the septum dividing the sides of the heart (VSD), it may have been even longer before the problem was discovered. This is because the oxygenated & unoxygenated blood could mix. This is explained better on page 10..

Matty's arteries (pipes that carry blood from the heart) were backwards. This is called TGV (Transposition of the Great Vessels). If you are older and would like to learn about a normal heart and Matty's heart when he was born, go to the next page with your parents. Without surgery Matty would have died. The doctor had to switch the arteries (pipes) around so the heart would work right. If you are little, jump with me (Mr. Pump) right over to page 11.

There is a new drug that was brought into use in the 1980's that keeps the ductus arteriosus open until surgery or corrective measures can be made. It is called prostaglandin E1. In Matty's case, he had an emergency balloon atrial septostomy, hole made in his septum dividing the right and left atrium of his heart at 2 days old, and open heart corrective surgery done at 10 days old. The prostaglandin E1 gave the doctors some time to stabilize Matty before beginning these critical procedures.

1) PROSTAGLANDIN: This drug is one of a family of acidic lipids that occur naturally in the body. It causes vasodilation (relaxing of the blood vessels), and the ductus arteriosus is especially sensitive to this drug. In infants (especially under 4 days old), 50% will see an increase in blood oxygen saturation of 23%. The infusion has to be given continuously, because 80% of the drug is lost when it passes through the body.

Side Effects:

Fever	— 14%
Apnea (stop breathing)	— 12%
Rash	— 10%
Slow heart beat	— 7%
Seizures	— 4%
Low blood pressure	— 4%
Fast heart beat	— 3%
Diarrhea	— 2%

Long term cancer and fertility studies have not been done
1) Reference from 1994 PDR (Physician Desk Reference) page 2441

NORMAL BIRTH HEART

See upper heart on right, how the blood goes from the body & brain - right side of the heart - through the Pulmonary Artery - to the lungs (where it receives oxygen) - to the left side of the heart - to the Aorta - back to the body.

MATTY'S BIRTH HEART

In the picture below you can see the patent ductus arteriosus, this is part of the fetal circulation and allows the blood with oxygen to mix with the blood without oxygen. Normally within a few hours after birth, it starts closing. When it is completely closed and if there aren't any other abnormalities that allows the blood to mix, the baby will die.

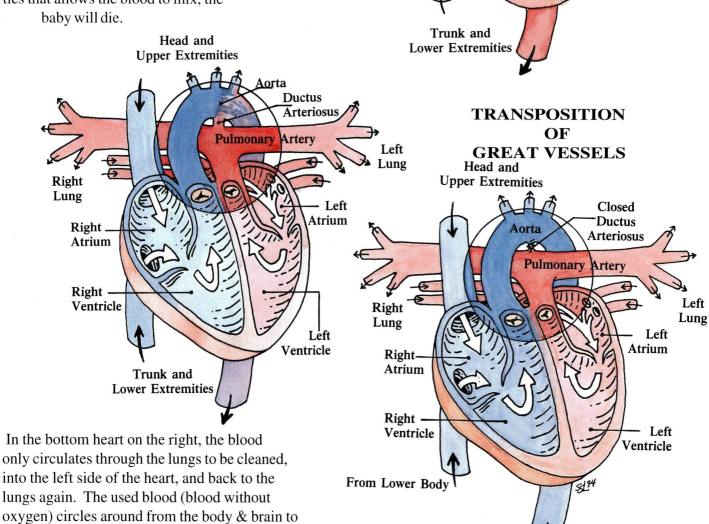

In the bottom heart on the right, the blood only circulates through the lungs to be cleaned, into the left side of the heart, and back to the lungs again. The used blood (blood without oxygen) circles around from the body & brain to the right side of the heart and back to the body & brain. The blood is never able to receive oxygen.

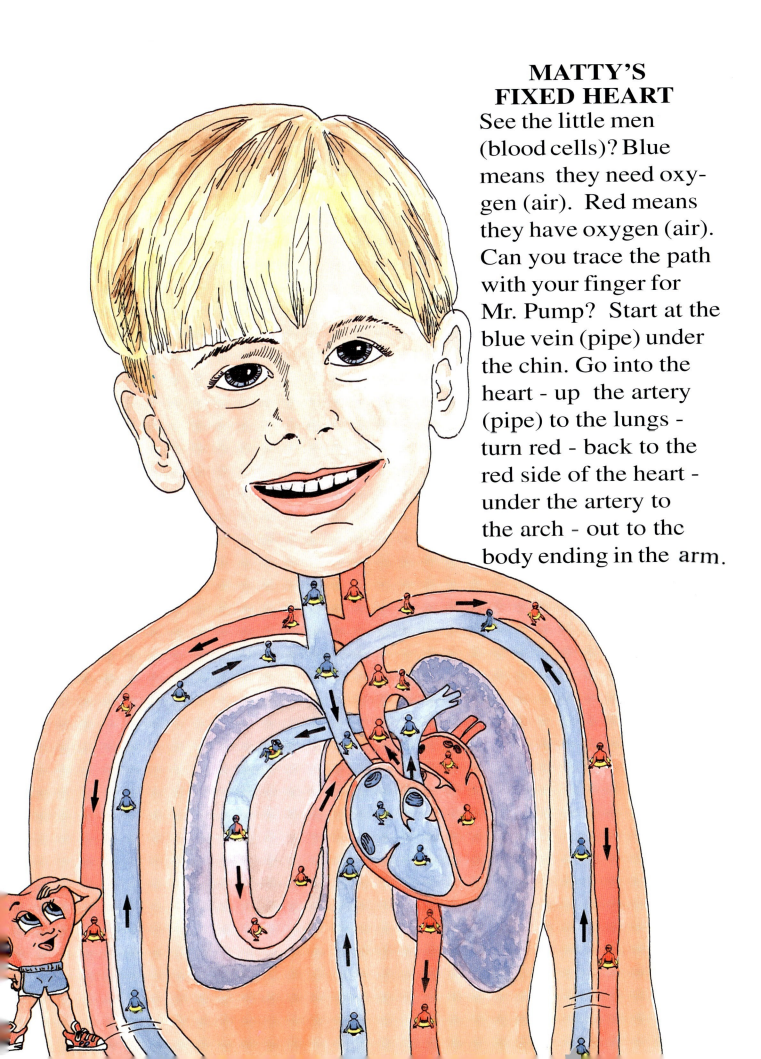

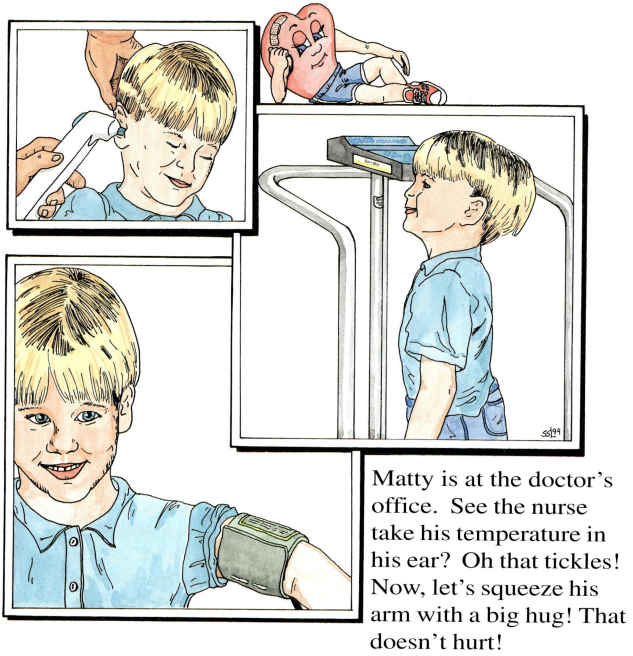

Matty is at the doctor's office. See the nurse take his temperature in his ear? Oh that tickles! Now, let's squeeze his arm with a big hug! That doesn't hurt!

Stand straight and tall on the scales Matty so we can see how big you are.

"I'm a big boy now," said Matty. "Not a baby."

Children with preexisting cardiac problems will probably be followed by the cardiologist on a regular basis. The doctor will establish a schedule of visits that are best suited for your child's condition. It is essential to keep these appointments even if your child seems OK. Cardiac conditions in children don't always have any signs or symptoms until the condition is quite advanced. Children's bodies have an amazing way of compensating. In my grandson's case, we have gone in for a routine exam, or had a heart cath that was to be routine, only to find out he had a potential life threatening condition. He has even surprised the cardiologists. So, I stress again, these follow-up appointments are essential.

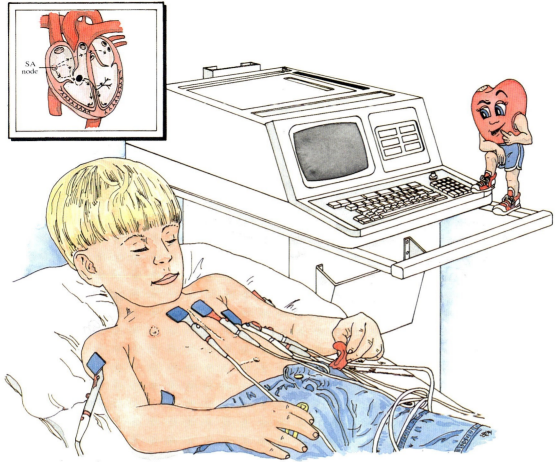

See me standing on the EKG machine? Hmm, which button should I push? See the blue squares with wires on Matty's chest and arm?

"It won't hurt, I promise." Said the nurse.

"You're right, no owees" Matty said. "Boy, you're done already?"

Matty needs the EKG to make sure his heart is beating right.

EKG or ECG (electrocardiogram) is a graphic representation of the electrical activity of the heart. A 12 lead EKG shows electrical activity from different angles. It is this electrical activity that causes the heart to contract or beat. From the EKG the doctor can tell how fast the heart is beating and how long it takes the electrical current to get from one section of the heart to the other. In general, children do not have life threatening disturbances of electrical pathways of the heart as the primary problem. Instead, it is normally a secondary problem or complication. The SA node is a node at the junction of the superior vena cave and the right atrium. This SA node is what initiates the electrical activity, and sends it out to the rest of the heart (see above illustration). The EKG/ECG is a measure of how electricity travels and how the heart responds to it. If the child lies very still, it is a painless procedure that lasts less than a couple of minutes.

Peek-a-Boo! I see you Echocardiogram Lady!

"Now Matty you have to lay very still. If you can't we will have to give you some medicine to make you sleep. I think you are a big enough boy to lie still. All I will do is squirt this cold jelly on your chest and rub it around with this stick — No owee's. Do you think you can lay still?" Said the lady in the white coat. Matty shakes his head yes.

"You can watch your heart on the TV monitor, we are even going to video tape it. Now, lets watch the blood swish through your heart on the TV." Said the lady.

"I'm a little scared, can my Mommy stay in the room?" Asked Matty.

"Sure" said the lady in the white coat.

"BrrrrBrrrr" said Matty as she squirted the jelly on his chest. See, he's laying very still with his Mommy sitting next to him. "Wow! That looks really neat! That didn't hurt — but it sure took a long time," Matty said.

"You were a very brave boy for holding still — here is a sticker," said the lady in the white coat.

"Oh thank you" said Matty.

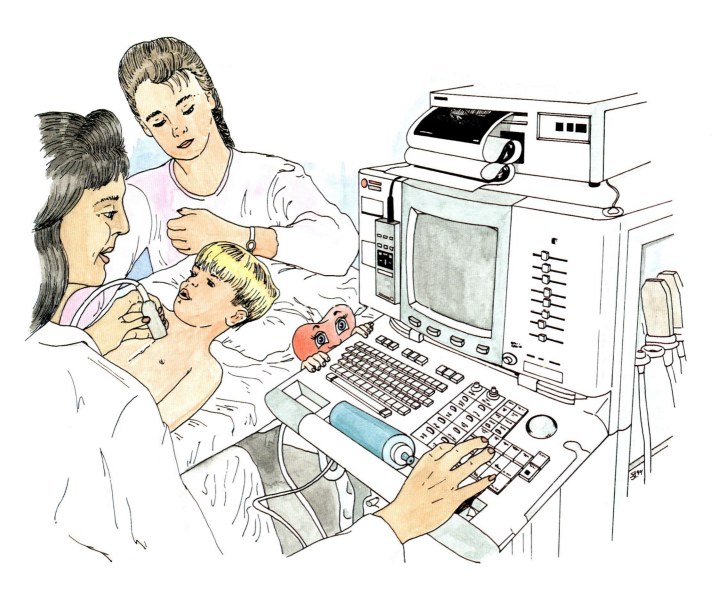

The echocardiogram is also a painless procedure. It is an ultrasound of the heart. Very small children are normally given medication to make them sleep through the procedure. Many doctors use chloral hydrate. Because of the bitter taste it is often a challenge to get the child to take it. It is then best to turn off the lights and TV and try to get your child asleep. Some children will have the opposite reaction and become extremely hyperactive. If this occurs you will need to guard your child from injury very carefully. They will not have much coordination or control. The echocardiogram shows the blood flowing through the heart and can detect narrowing of the arteries, back flow through the valves, thickening of the septum or walls of the heart, holes in the septum, etc. Since it is a painless procedure many children, by the time they are 3 - 5 years old, will not need to be medicated. You will probably be a good judge of whether or not your child can lie still for that long.

Oh, this is scary. Matty's Mommy looks like she was crying, so Matty feels a little scared. Lets listen to Matty's doctor.

"Matty," the doctor said "Your heart is not working right. See this picture, these two arteries (Aorta and Pulmonary), are like pipes that take blood from the heart. Yours are getting smaller, and we need to make them bigger."

"Little owee" Matty said.

"Matty, it will be a big owee," Mommy said. "The doctor will give you some medicine when it hurts."

"No owee!" Matty shouted and started to cry.

"Matty, I'm sorry but we have to. You will have to be very brave," Mommy said and hugged him.

"We will put you to sleep to do it, then give medicine afterwards for pain. When you are put to sleep you won't wake up until we wake you up," said the doctor. "You will have it done at the hospital, and your mommy and daddy can stay with you."

When the doctor gives you this type of information, it is like someone has hit you with a truck. A child will take his clue from you on how to respond. He knows you and will probably sense that something is wrong. It is best to be honest. Explain matter-of-factly to your child what the problem is to the best of his understanding. The two big concerns a child will have are pain and separation from parents. Reassure them in both cases, in fact you will probably need to emphasize it over and over again. Children who must go through very traumatic surgeries/procedures, do best with support and love. A hospital is a scary place even for an adult. Kids may get scared sombody will sneak up on them and thus they can never relax. So it is important to reassure them that if anything will hurt you will tell them first. If there is anyway at all, arrange your schedule to spend most of your time with your child. The younger your child, the more important this is.

You are their only form of security. Again I stress, be honest with them. If something will hurt, tell them, then let them know you will hold their hand through it. Let them know it is OK to cry. They must hold still. If you lie to them, they won't feel safe and may not trust you. If they know when you say it won't hurt, it won't, they will be much more cooperative. Fear of the unknown is scary to all of us. This hospitalization, though traumatic, will build a bond between you and your child. It will show him you will always be there. Trial builds character, and this will build character in you and your child. You will be surprised how strong you can be.

Let's watch Matty having a heart cath. Do you know what a heart cath is? It is where a very small tube is put into an artery in the top of the leg, and threaded up to the heart. This is a better way to check the heart.

"Matty, drink this medicine" says the nurse. "It will make you sleepy, so you will sleep through the heart cath and it won't hurt." See Matty drinking his medicine like a good boy?

"UK!" Said Matty.

Shhh! He is sleeping now. See he is in the heart cath room. See picture A? That is the catheter (tube) they use, with a balloon on it. He won't wake up till he's back in bed with his Mommy right beside him.

"Is it done?" Matty said.

"You're all done Matty" Mommy said. "You need to lie still for 6 hours so you don't make your leg start bleeding. We will be staying here tonight so they can fix your heart tomorrow."

A heart cath is a procedure usually done as a same day procedure or overnight stay. In some facilities anesthesia is given, others just medicate with a sedative like Chloral Hydrate. The procedure consists of placing a small very long tube into an artery and/or vein in the groin area at the top of the thigh. It is then threaded up to the heart. Video or film is taken of its progress up. It can check how the blood flows through the heart/lungs, and can measure accurate pressures of the blood flow. A common complication in children who have had open heart surgery at a young age, is that their arteries don't grow at the suture line. This causes a narrowing of the artery and an increase in pressure, as the blood pushes against this narrow area (Like 4 lanes of heavy traffic merging into a single lane - it causes backups). Sometimes they can use catheters with little balloons at the tip. After the catheter is in the narrowing, they slowly blow up the balloon to stretch the area. They are also using stents (a small wire tube, like a roll of chicken wire collapsed) that are placed on the tube over the balloon. They place the stents wherever needed, blow up the balloon that stretches out the stent. They leave the stent in the child to keep the artery open. Heart caths are used for both diagnosis and treatment.

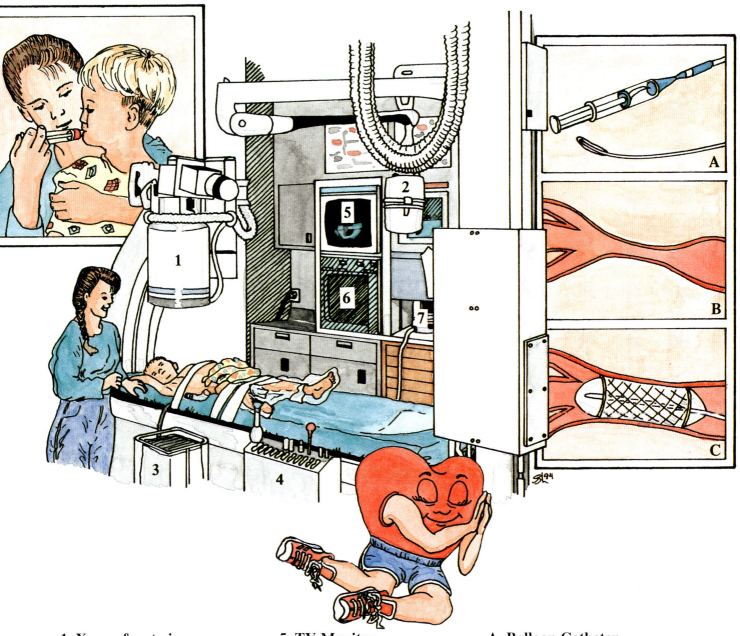

1. Xray - front view
2. Xray - side view
3. Record box
4. Control panel
5. TV Monitor
6. Heart Monitor
7. Oximeter

A. Balloon Catheter
B. constricted artery before
C. artery after with stent, before balloon catheter removed.

After the heart cath, it is extremely important that the child lay still for a minimum of 6 hours. Bring quiet toys that can be played with from a laying down position (example hand held video games, little cars or people, books etc.). If your child starts to bleed from the cath insert area they will probably apply pressure, or at least a pressure bandage. If your child won't stay quiet or keep the legs straight and still, they may have to medicate with a sedative. Next, it is important to push fluids, unless vomiting is present. They will probably have to check the hematocrit before discharging home. Hematocrit is a simple blood test to make sure your child hasn't lost too much blood or isn't bleeding internally. When you go home your child will need to take it easy for 2 or 3 days (no sports or rough housing). If he starts bleeding from the site, or the site becomes red and inflamed, or he develops a temperature, you need to call your doctor.

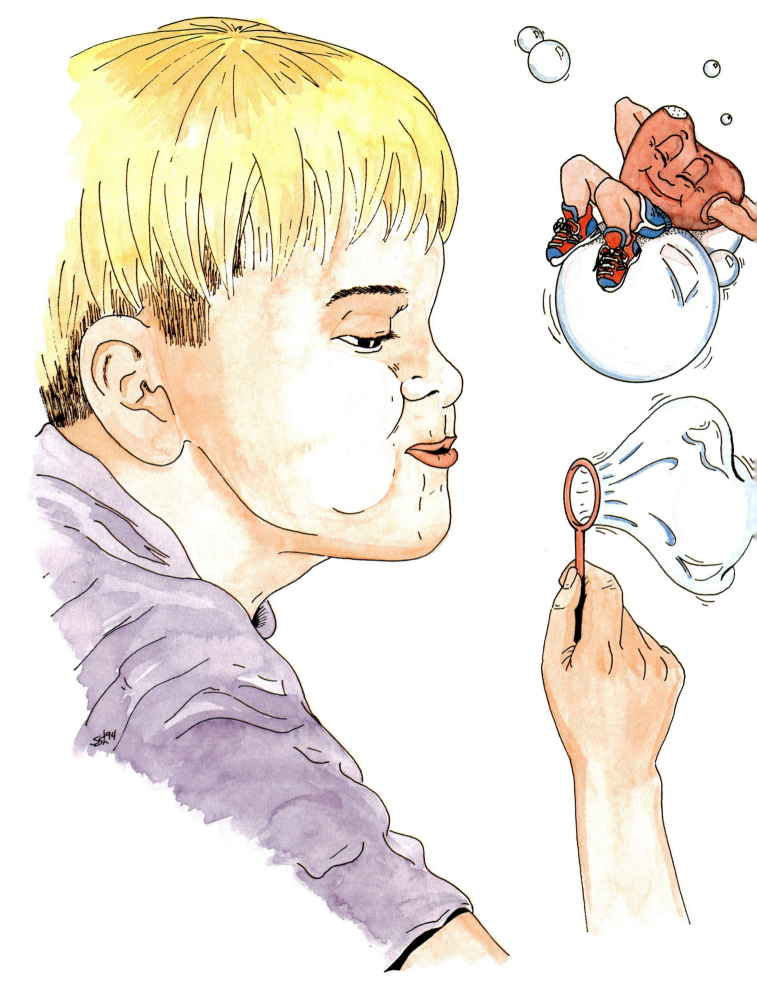

Oh Bubbles! I love blowing bubbles, don't you?

The nurse is talking to Matty and his Mommy about the surgery. She's explaining about the tubes, IV's, and the monitors to watch his heart beating.

"Matty you will probably have your hands tied to the side of the bed. It's not because you are bad, but because when you're sleeping you might accidently pull out a tube and hurt yourself" said the nurse. "It might hurt, even with the medicine, when the nurse moves you in bed, or if you move yourself. You need to blow like this" and she shows him. "Count to 3, then move yourself blowing 4 or 5 times. That will help it stop hurting. Think of blowing bubbles and watching your favorite toy."

Matty likes to blow bubbles. Look at me floating up, up in the air!

The nurse will come in the night before to explain what to expect after surgery. The doctor will explain the actual surgery itself. Pain can be a major concern with such a surgery, as you can't really make a child totally pain free. First, don't allow the pain to get real bad before asking for pain medication. It often takes much more pain medication to get the pain under control if you wait to long. Certain things, such as moving or turning in bed, do hurt. This is essential for preventing pneumonia. I think most people are familiar with Lamaze breathing, this concept of blowing is the same (set a focal point, stare at it, and blow a few times or take slow deep breaths). This helps the focus to be on something else rather than the pain. A very young child probably will not understand this concept, but after about age 3, especially if practiced ahead of time, they probably will. You will need to continue to remind them or even blow with them. This blowing of course will not be able to be done until after the breathing tube is out of the mouth. When the nurse comes in for the preop teaching it is your time to ask any specific questions you may have. Write them down as you think of them, so you won't forget when she comes in.

That night Matty said, "Mommy will I die?"

"Oh Matty," said Mommy, as her eyes filled with tears. "The doctor said there is only a small chance of that."

"Mommy I don't want to leave you and Daddy!" And Matty started to cry.

"I don't want you to leave either, and you probably won't die," said Mommy. "However, if you do die Matty, you won't ever be hurt again. Your heart won't be broken anymore. You love our Lord. I can promise you will go to heaven to be with Him. Your two great Grandmas are in heaven and they will all take care of you till Daddy and I can come to heaven to be with you. I know it is scary, but we have to trust in our Lord, to do what is best for you."

"Mommy I'm scared!" Said Matty.

"I'm a little scared too, but I know you will be OK," said Mommy. "I love you very much."

"I love you too, Mommy," Matty said and gave his Mommy a big hug.

"Now let's practice your blowing, for when you wake up after surgery," said Mommy.

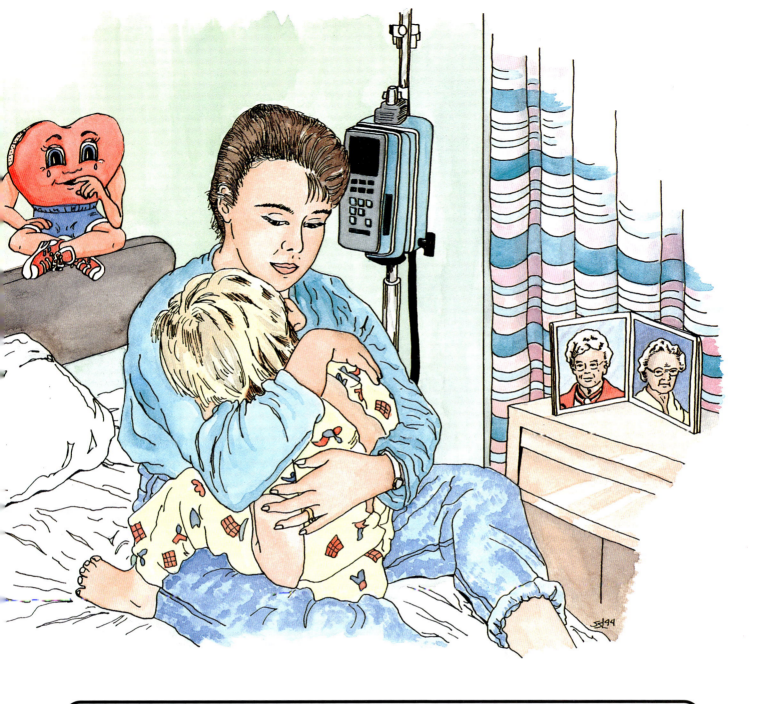

I have heard children as young as 3 ask about dying, in fact this conversation took place when Matt was 3. A young child may view dying differently, more fear of separation from parents and family. Older children understand more the finality/reality of death. You can't face open heart surgery and not face death. You also can't promise they won't die. If they are old enough to understand percentages the doctor will probably give you a percentage. If it is 2 - 3%, stress that it's 97 - 98% they will live. Stress the positive. Talk about dying from a positive point of view. Be honest with your feeling. If you feel scared or sad, it is OK to share that with them. It gives them permission to be honest with their feelings, and it shows them your love. Crying is a natural release. You can even cry together. I cry the night before each of my grandson's surgeries or procedures, not knowing if he will be with us the next night or not. After a short time of talking, crying and praying about the possibility of dying, turn your focus on preparing for after surgery and living. Keeping your child busy the night before is important. After preparing for surgery, play video games, etc. with your child to help the evening go by faster. If at all possible, stay with them till they go to sleep or stay the night.

Orange Soap! Washing with orange soap, that's silly. The orange soap kills the germs (bad bugs) on the skin. Don't worry, it comes off. Matty won't stay orange.

"Mommy can I have a drink or some breakfast?" Matty asked.

"No," said Mommy, "You can't have anything before surgery except medicine. Remember? The nurse told you last night."

"But I'm hungry!" Cried Matty

"I know" said Mommy, "let's watch cartoons. Oh here comes your nurse."

"Take this medicine Matty, it will make you sleepy like yesterday," said the nurse.

See Matty sleeping on Daddys' lap with ME! Even Daddy is sleeping.

Your child will be NPO (nothing by mouth) probably after midnight. It actually depends on the time of day your child's surgery will be. The reason for this is, they want the stomach empty in case of vomiting. Since your child will be under heavy anesthesia, there is a danger of aspirating (sucking vomitus into the lungs). Don't even allow your child to brush his teeth, unless you are sure they are old enough not to swallow any fluid. The orange soap is an iodine type of substance to help remove bacteria (germs) off the skin. It is not uncommon to take a bath with this 2 times (evening before and morning of surgery). Preop medication depends on the anesthesiologist and his routine. Normally, in my experience, I have seen only a shot given of a narcotic and a medication to help dry up saliva. Once, my grandson was given a very small amount of a liquid to drink, instead of a shot, before he was taken to surgery. Your child will have to wear a hospital gown to the OR. Many places will not allow the child to wear their underwear. This seems to be one of the more upsetting things for children. It is primarily so the underwear doesn't get lost, or thrown out with the OR linens. Also your child will not be able to wear jewelry, nail polish, barrettes, rubberbands that have any metal in them, retainers, contact lenses,

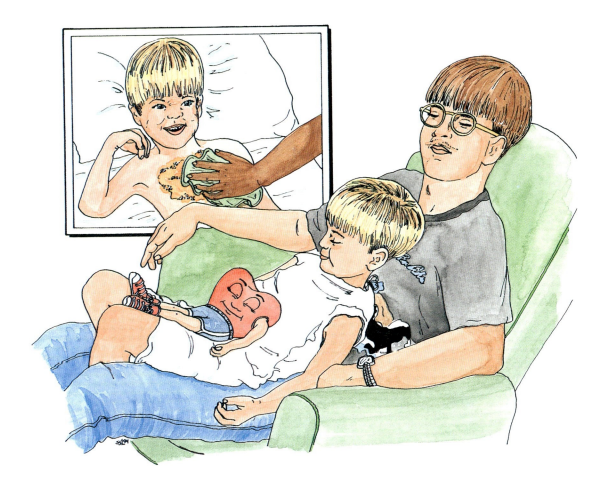

glasses etc., to the OR. Sometimes an IV is put in before surgery, but not always. Talk with your doctor and anesthesiologist about what their routine is, so you can explain and prepare your child. Once again, if something is going to hurt tell them ahead of time. Once they have your trust on this, they will stay calm for the non - painful procedures and know you will help them through the painful ones. With my grandson we even rate the procedures: little oowee (blood draw) / oowee (IV start) / big oowee (surgical pain). Your child when ready for surgery, will go on a gurney. He may or may not be asleep. You will be allowed to walk to the OR with him, but won't be able to go into the surgical suite. It can be a very long wait. It takes up to an hour to prepare your child before surgery even starts. Matt's longest surgery was approximately 9 hours, and the shortest was about 3 1/2 hours. While you wait, walk around the hospital, go to the gift shop and browse, play cards. One time my daughter cleaned a stuffed animal that had gotten gross, but Matt wouldn't part from it. So she took this time to wash and blow dry it in the hospital. Make sure you use this time to eat. You will need your strength after your child comes back, and it may be harder to get away. Notify a nurse when you leave the waiting area so they can page you if there is a problem and they need to talk to you. Sitting and worrying won't change anything and it will make you a nervous wreck. Keep in mind that no news is good news, 99% of the time.

See Matty waking up? Oh this is scary!

"Matty," Daddy said "You have the tube in your mouth so you can't talk. Remember the Nurse told you about it? You are OK and your heart is all fixed. We love you."

Matty hears beeping and swishing sounds. The swishing is the ventilator to help Matty to breathe. See the breathing tube in the picture?

"Matty your hands are tied down so you can't forget and pull out your IV lines or your tubes" Mommy said. "Go back to sleep, you are ok."

Matty will go to sleep, because the nurse gave him some medicine.

We can only imagine the terror a child must feel on awakening. The infant and toddler the most, because they go on feelings only and just don't understand what's happening. Your child will probably be kept medicated. When I awoke from my surgery I was amazed at how fully awake I was. Talk to him as if he understands everything you say. When you talk with each other, the nurse or the doctor, keep in mind he may be listening to everything you say. Explain everything you or the nurses are doing as if he hears and understands everything. He just may, even if he appears to be asleep. The ICU is a scary, noisy place, try to be with your child as much as possible. Remember you are your child's only sense of security. Hospitals are becoming much more relaxed in allowing you to stay with your child. My daughter, son-in-law and I have even done shifts sitting at the bedside, until he gets out of the ICU, so he never has to be alone. Of course, not everyone can do this. With other children at home or without family support it can be impossible to stay. You can't let yourself get sick either. If you are alone with your child, ask the nurse to wake or call you if your child awakens or is scared. You need to take care of yourself, in order to have the strength to care for your child. Talk with your child about this ahead of time, sometimes just knowing you are sleeping nearby or a phone call away, is enough for the child to not be afraid. Just talk with the night nurse ahead of time, and let her know under what circumstances you want to be awaken. Your child will come back from OR on a ventilator. First, the trauma to the area from surgery could potentially make respiration's difficult or even cease. Second, by the respirator doing the breathing, the heart doesn't have to work so hard. It is important to put as little stress on the heart as possible, for healing to occur. The tube in the mouth is the best way to deliver the air to the lungs. Since air is prevented from going past the voice box it is impossible to talk or make noise. This in itself is frustrating. If your child is old enough, teach him a couple of signs to make with his fingers. Stress to your child that this is all only temporary.

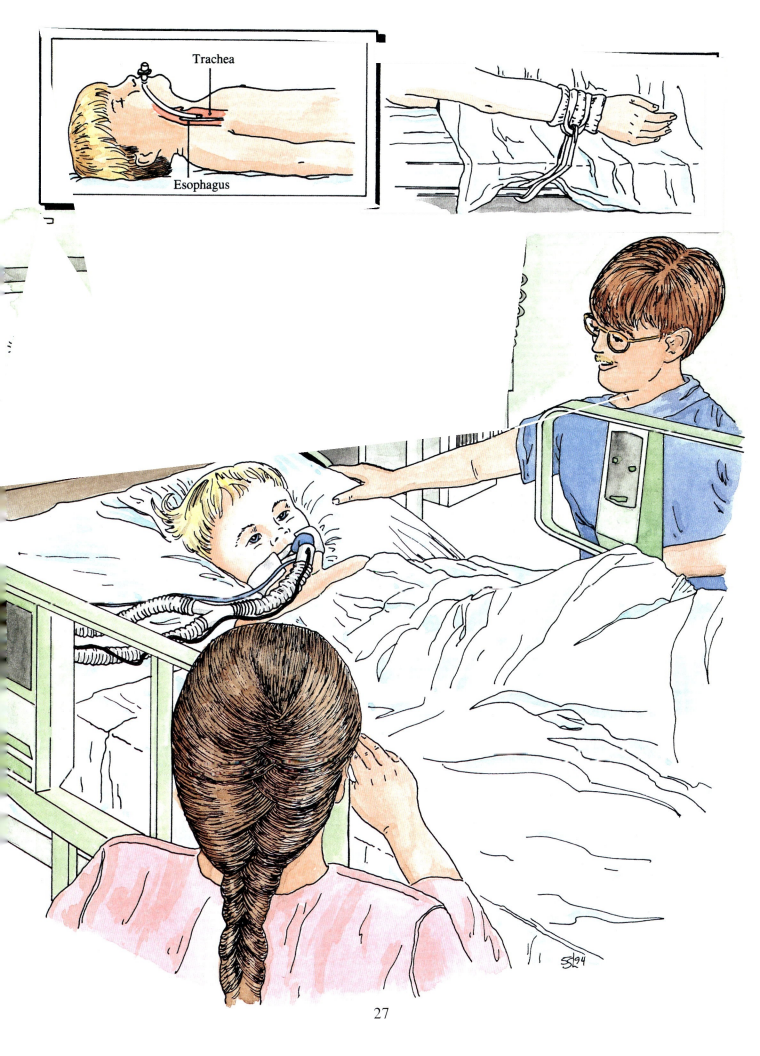

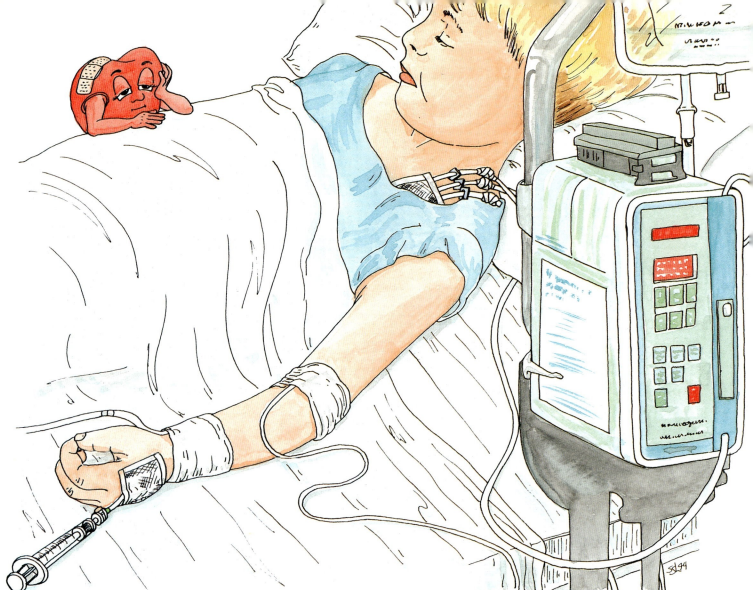

Oh look at the IV's. Wow I see 1..2..3..4 here. IV's are for drawing blood, giving medicine and giving Matty fluid (water). Now Matty won't need to be poked any more. No OWEEEES! If Matty pulls them out, he will need to be poked to put them back in. OUCH! Matty, don't touch your IV's!

> Your child will probably have even more lines than what is actually shown here. All medications are given through the IV line. Once in, the IV may be a little uncomfortable with certain medications, but they should not actually hurt. It will look very complicated, with all the stopcocks, syringes etc. These lines are also used to draw all the blood samples and blood gases they need. Some lines are in the arteries, some into veins, and they will probably have a central line into the heart itself, or a great vessel. If you ever notice any swelling or redness at these sites, please let your nurse know right away. Medications vary greatly from institution to institution, doctor to doctor, and what your child's specific condition is. If you want to know about the medications your child is on, ask the nurse to have the pharmacy give you printouts on the medication. The nurse herself may have basic information about the drug and why your child is on it. Don't be afraid to ask questions, this is your child and you have a right to know.

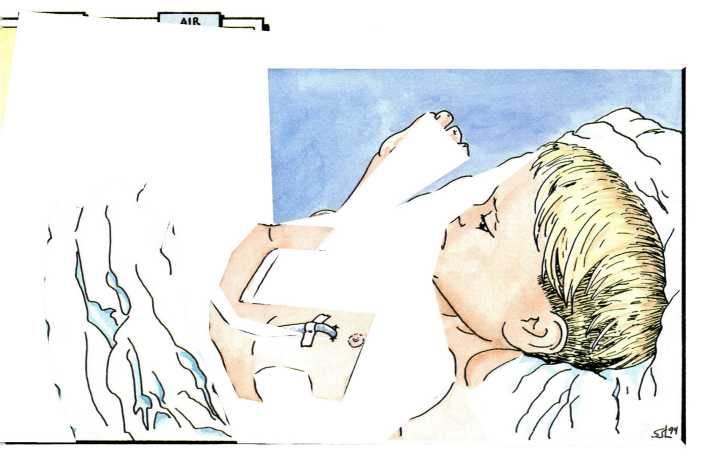

See Matty's chest tubes? One was left uncovered so you can see where it goes. These, like the IV's, were put in while Matty was sleeping in surgery. Putting them in did not hurt. The chest tubes drain the extra water and fluid in the chest, so Matty can breathe easier.

in the pleural cavity. In normal respiration, without surgery, the air rushes into your lungs because of a negative pressure in your lungs compared to the atmosphere around you. When the pressure in your lungs becomes greater than the air (atmosphere) around you, then you exhale the air out. With fluid and blood around your lungs it is difficult to breathe. To see why, imagine you have a glass bottle with a balloon in it, as in diagram A above. If you have air and water in the bottle, it would be difficult to blow up the balloon very much. If you had another tube in the bottle that sucked out all the air and fluid as in diagram B, then you could blow up the balloon. This is how the chest tubes work. The balloon is like your lungs, and the bottle is like your body. Matt typically has two chest tubes in, one on each side. At first the drainage will probably be quite bloody looking, but should become clearer as time goes by. Matt's chest tubes stay in typically two to three days. The Chest tubes will be placed in surgery. There is pain on milking the tubes, fluid collects in the line and you milk it down the tube so it will go into the container. There is definitely pain when the tube is removed. You may want to make sure your child has had some pain medication before this. After the chest tube is out, the pain quickly goes away. Just remember, you are one step closer to going home.

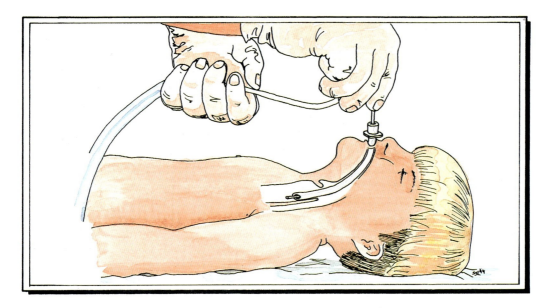

"Matty, I have to suction you through the tube in your mouth," said the nurse. "You will cough when I suction you."

Do you like to drink soda through a straw? I do. When you suck up, the soda goes in your mouth. Yummy, yummy in your tummy! When the nurse suctions you, she sucks up the mucous (runny nose stuff) in your breathing tube. It's real yukkie, but she has to get it out so you can breathe. Just like you have to blow your nose when it runs. Matty, squeeze Daddy's hand when she suctions you, it will be over in just a minute.

"Good Boy Matty! I know that was hard," said the nurse.

Shh, Matty's going to sleep holding Daddy's hand.

> Suctioning, to me, was the worst part of the surgery. I think Matt must have felt the same, because he would cry when the suction machine was turned on. First, they disconnect you from the respirator. Sometimes they will place a few drops of normal saline (salt water) down your breathing tube. They do this to loosen the secretions or mucous. If they do, they will put you back on the respirator to mix the water with the mucous. Then they suction it out. If they do not suction, fluid and mucous will collect in the airway, until you can no longer breathe. As you can see, it is a very necessary procedure. After the tube is out, and your child is off the respirator, it is very important for your child to cough those secretions out. Turning your child from side to side will also aid in keeping the lungs cleared out. It keeps mucous from pooling in one area of the lung, which occurs when in one position too long. A chest X-ray will be taken frequently to monitor how the lungs are doing. Stress that the tube and suctioning are temporary.

See the last two tubes? These are also placed in surgery, so no owee. The tube in Matty's nose keeps his tummy empty, so he won't throw up. Matty has a little sore throat, it will go away after the tube is gone. The tube in Matty's bladder drains the pee, so that he won't have to go potty. When it comes out he can go pee like he always did. It burns a little at first, then goes away.

Shhh! Matty, go to sleep, you're ok.

> With the tube in the airway, the last thing you would want is your child vomiting. It would probably force the airway tube out, and could compromise his respiratory status. The tube into the nose is also placed in surgery and is attached to suction. This will keep your child's stomach empty. Once in place, it is a little uncomfortable but with everything else, it is hardly noticed. It may cause your child to gag when pulled out, but once gone, that is it. Urine output monitoring is very critical, so a catheter (foley) is placed into the bladder and the balloon is inflated to keep it in. If your child retains fluid, this will make his heart have to work a lot harder to push it around, and his lungs work harder to breathe around it. It may be necessary to give your child some medicine called Furosemide to pull the fluid out of the tissues so he can pee it out. Furosemide is a diuretic (a stronger form of water pill like medication). Given by IV it will peak in 20 - 60 minutes. Furosemide should be given slowly, over 1 - 2 minutes. If Furosemide is given too quickly, hearing loss can occur. Other side effects are: Volume depletion, dehydration, hypokalemia (low potassium), fluid/electrolyte imbalances. Your child will be monitored for these potential problems very closely.

Look Matty's sleeping right now. See how he looks right after surgery? I know it looks scary, but Matty is ok. Each day the doctor or nurse will take out different lines or tubes. It means he's getting better.

The first time we saw Matt after his first open heart surgery was quite traumatic. This small little child, with all these tubes and lines, even as a nurse it was so hard to see. He was on an adult gurney (to make room for all the equipment) and looked so small and defenseless.

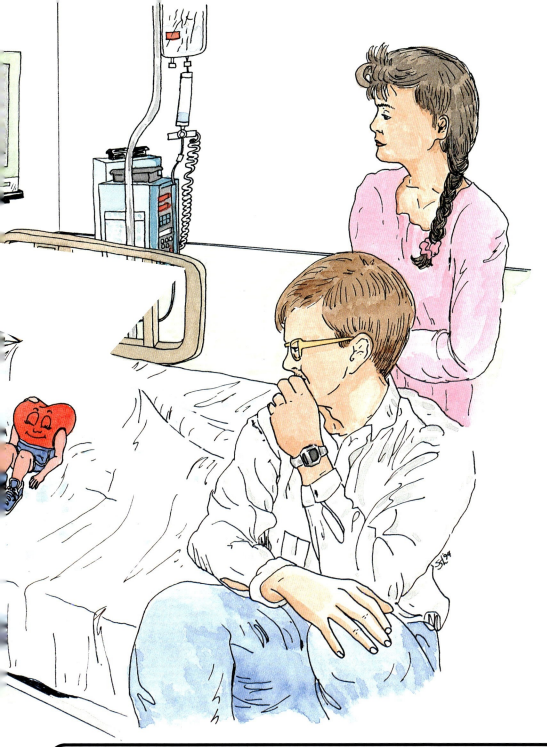

The heart lung machine can make your body retain fluid, so your child may look puffy. The younger the child, the more swollen they may look. Within a day or so you may see a dramatic improvement. I haven't shown the pacemaker wires. It is just 2 wires that can be attached to an external pacemaker. The heart is sometimes swollen and sluggish after surgery and needs temporary help to beat properly. Matt has never needed to use these in his first 3 surgeries. He had an internal pacemaker in his fourth surgery. In this picture: the respirator is on the left of the bed, the suction canisters are at the head of the bed, the monitor is also at the head of the bed, and the IV pumps are on each side of the bed. The patches on the chest are monitor leads. The Dressing is in the center of the chest. The chest tube container is hanging on the side of the bed. The foley (urine) bag is next to the left chest tube container. The ambu bag is on his pillow. The ambu bag is to help him breathe when he is off the respirator. ICU's and equipment vary, but you can get a general idea.

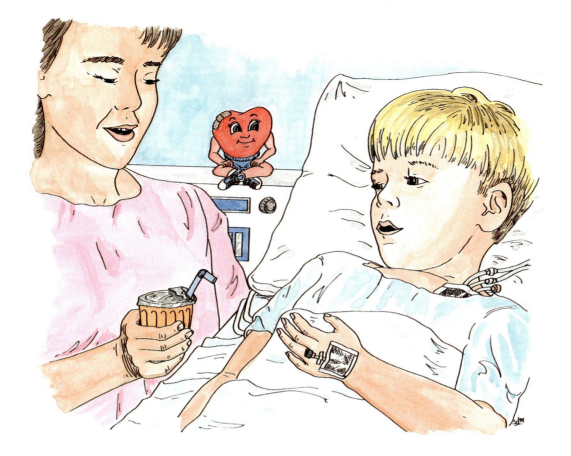

Oh Look! The doctors took out Matty's breathing and nose tube. Matty is whispering. Don't worry his voice will come back before today is over. See how happy he is? Remember, each time they take something away, it means he's GETTING BETTER!

" Here is some apple juice," said Mommy. "Drink it slowly at first."

"Mommy, am I all better yet?" Matty asked after he sat up.

"Almost Matty, almost," said Mommy.

The breathing tube in the mouth can come out in 1 to 2 days or longer. Again, your child may gag when it is taken out. The tube in the nose may also come out at that time. Oxygen may be necessary after the ET tube is removed (breathing tube). If oxygen is necessary it will probably be given via mask or nasal cannula. It will be based on oxygen saturation's and the lungs. Oxygen saturation's will probably be shown on the monitor. On an average, I would say 70% - 92% as a low. Cardiac conditions accept much lower oxygen saturations than respiratory children, because oxygen doesn't change saturations much in cardiac children. Your doctor will determine what is best for your child and his condition. Coughing is one of the most important things to do at this time, it helps keep the lungs clear. Remember, each time something is taken away, you are one step closer to going home.

Wow, look at Matty! He walked down to the playroom! See all his IV's and tubes are gone, Yea! Matty loves to play video games.

"Matty what are you playing?" Asked the child life specialist.

"Games," Matty said. "Watch this!"

"I'm sure glad you're better," the child life specialist said.

"I'm all better!" Matty said.

> With Matt's 4th surgery he actually got to go to the playroom on the 4th day. Most children's hospital playrooms don't allow any procedures to occur in the playroom. That is the child's safe place, where they can relax. The sooner a child can return to normal activity, the quicker and more fully they will recover. Walking is a great form of exercise and will help the lungs clear and stay clear. Children seldom have to be encouraged to walk or play. In fact, the opposite is normally true, it's harder to keep them quiet. Many doctors are now placing children on low fat diets to reduce fluid retention or effusion (fluid collecting around the outside of the heart and/or lungs). Talk with your doctor to see if this is right for your child.

"Matty," the doctor said, "Would you like to go home today— you look great." Matty's going home after seven days, Hooray!

"Oh yes, yes, yes!" Yelled Matty.

"You should be very proud, you have done a good job. You are a very brave little boy. Thank you for being so good," said the doctor, "OK, you can go home today. No sports or rough housing; you can play, but you need to be careful not to fall on your chest."

"I promise" said Matty.

"Now you must call me if you feel sleepy or tired all the time, if your finger tips or nail beds look blue, if you have trouble breathing, or if you have sudden pain here," said the doctor pointing to Matty's chest.

"Oh I will, I will," said Matty as he clapped his hands.

Going home is the greatest, most exciting time. You've made it and have all done a great job. Since we are dealing with a cardiac problem, the doctor will tell you what to expect in your recovery. Guidelines you should know, if they haven't been addressed, are: 1. If not able to shower yet, find out when your child can shower or take a tub bath. 2. Know what temperature the doctor wants you to report immediately, if you child starts to run a fever. 3. When your child can start to participate in normal rough play. 4. How to care for the wound and how frequently. 5. Know your medications, side effects, dosages, and how often they are given. 6. Know what symptoms need to be reported immediately. 7. Know when you are expected to return to the doctor.
TAKE A CPR CLASS BEFORE TAKING YOUR CHILD HOME, IF YOU ARE NOT ALREADY CERTIFIED, AND EVERYONE WHO WILL BE ALONE WITH YOUR CHILD NEEDS TO KNOW CPR.

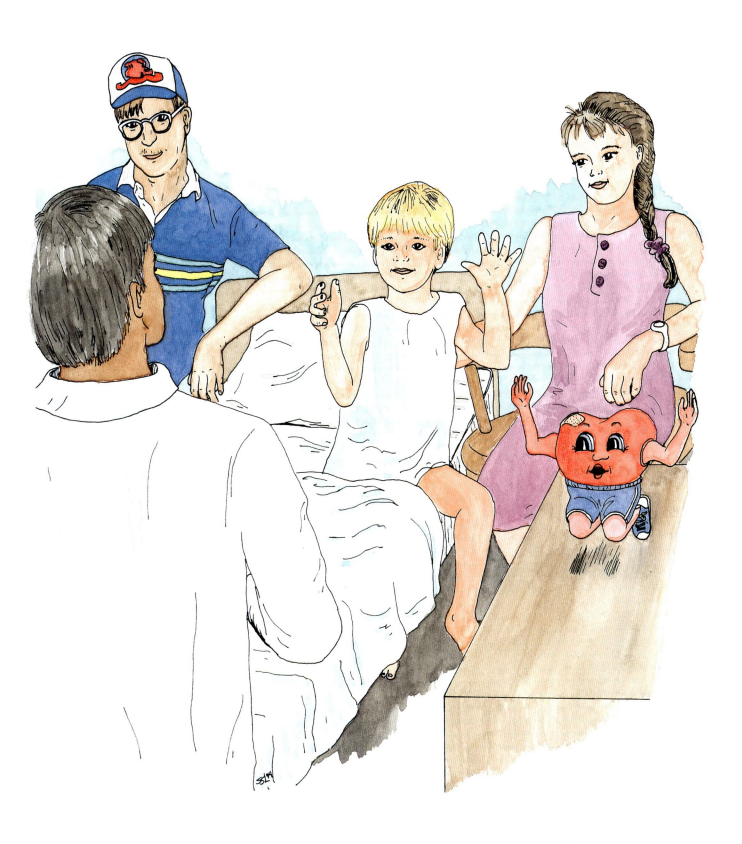

On Matt's 2nd and 3rd surgery, we noticed him always pulling his shirt away from his chest. We never understood why until I had my surgery. The nerve endings at times can be very sensitive, and it can bother you to have anything touch the skin. I walked around for a good month holding my shirt away from my skin. We have also been told that you should avoid sunlight to the scar area for a year afterwards, to lessen the scaring. This can be done easily by just wearing a shirt when outside or swimming.

Oh boy, lets play ball! It's been 2 months since Matty's surgery and look at him go. Do you think I can get the ball away from him? I don't think so.
Matty's favorite thing to do is play basketball with Daddy. He can now play just like all little boys and girls can. His heart is all fixed.

Tomorrow he starts a new adventure,

PRESCHOOL!

Boy will he have a story to tell about what he did this summer!

When getting home, try to return to normal activity and discipline as soon as possible. Children can be manipulators and use sympathy for their condition to get their parents to accept behavior they normally would never tolerate. This is not healthy for your child or the family. Your child will recover quicker if he is not treated as if he is sick. He does need to rest, just don't fall into the habit of babying him. He needs to be somewhat active to keep his lungs cleared out. We can understand that he may regress some in his behavior, this has been a traumatic experience. He may even be angry. If he is old enough, have him play out his feeling with dolls or wooden people. Let one be the nurse, doctor, mommy, daddy and himself. This is a constructive way for him to show his feelings and talk about those feelings. Let him hit the toy doctor or nurse. Don't let him hit the real mommy, daddy, or siblings without consequence. He may be angry, but there are appropriate and inappropriate ways of expressing his anger. Children are smart, and will quickly learn what they can and cannot do. A week or so after coming home from the hospital, when you have all recovered, have a party! Celebrate this Glorious time, you've all made it!

DIARY OF HOSPITAL STAY

> Remember this is only a temporary situation. This diary will show the milestones you will accomplish on the road to going home. Mark off each one as it is accomplished. If you or your child really hates something, write it in that section. This will aid in helping them talk about it or play it out with their dolls/people. If you or your child really like something, put that down also. You can always find something positive, even in heart surgery (example : a present, a nurse does something special for you, etc.). Make this a positive tool.

MILESTONES:

1. Out of surgery, how long did it take:_____

2. Date ET tube (Airway tube) removed:_____

3. Date NG tube (tube in nose) removed:_____

4. Date first able to drink (boy am I thirsty):_____

5. Date chest tubes come out:_____

6. Date Foley (tube in bladder) comes out: _____

7. Date Central Line and/or Arterial Line comes out: _____

8. Date first walked after surgery:_____

9. Date left ICU:_____

10. Date first allowed to eat FOOD:_____

11. Date all IV lines are out:_____

12. Date you can walk in halls or go to the PLAYROOM:_____

13. Date you get to go HOME:_____

NURSES:

_____   _____

_____   _____

_____   _____

List what you hated the most:

_____

_____

_____

_____

_____

List what you liked the best:

_____

_____

_____

_____

YOU DID A GREAT JOB YOUR DONE!

MATTY'S HEART

EDUCATIONAL ACTIVITY SECTION

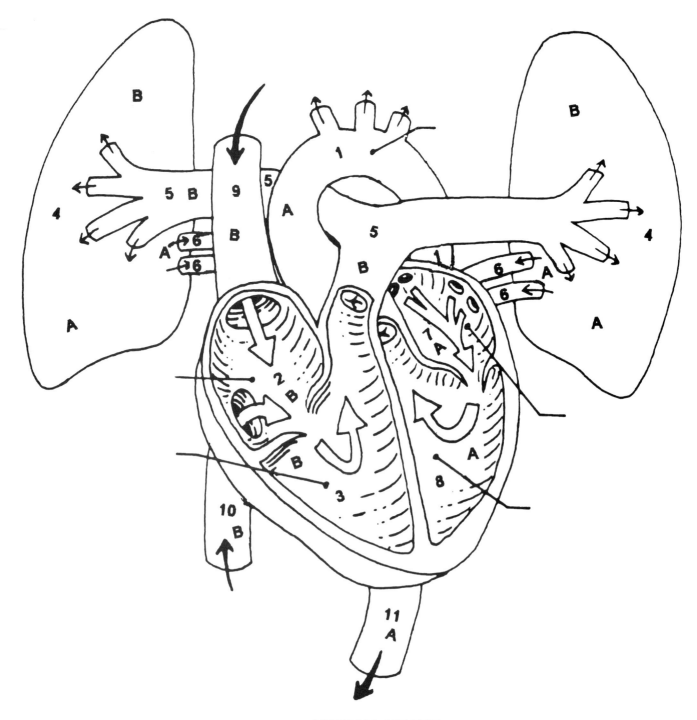

NORMAL HEART

Older child's instructions:
1. Aorta - Label picture and Color Red
2. Right Atrium - Label picture and Color Blue
3. Right Ventricle - Label picture and Color Blue
4. Lungs - Color part Blue and part Red
5. Pulmonary Artery - Color Blue
6. Pulmonary Veins - Color Red
7. Left Atrium - Color Red and label
8. Left Ventricle - Color Red and label
9. Superior Vena Cava - Color Blue
10. Inferior Vena Cava - Color Blue
11. Thoracic Aorta - Color Red

Young child's instruction
A. Color Red
B. Color Blue

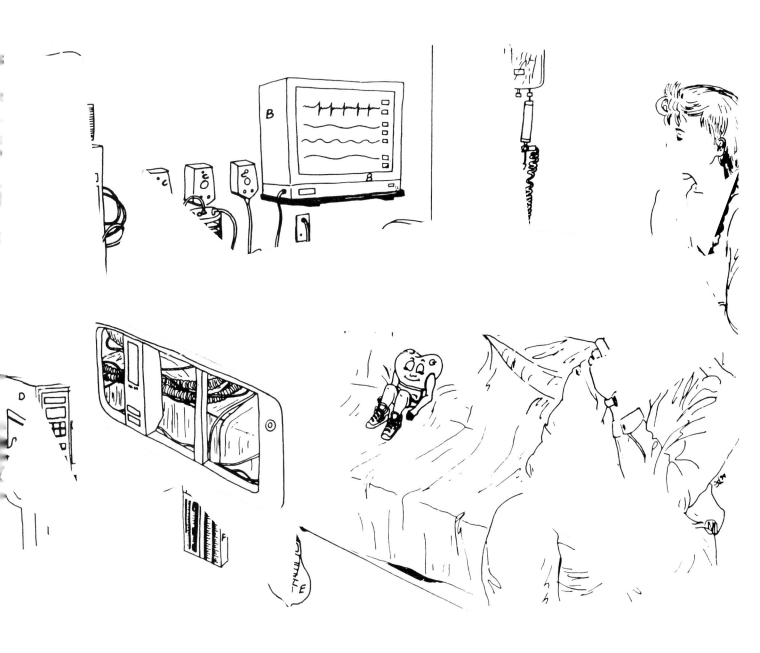

A. Respirator - helps me breath : Color Blue- color dials pretty colors
B. Monitor - to watch my heart beat: Color yellow with screen grey
C. Suction - to get the fluid out of me: Color tops red and cans white
D. IV Pumps - to give me water and medicine: Color purple
E. Foley - to help me pee: Color yellow
F. Chest tube cannister - to get out fluid around lungs: Color green
G. Mr. Pump - to help me learn about surgery: Color Red with blue

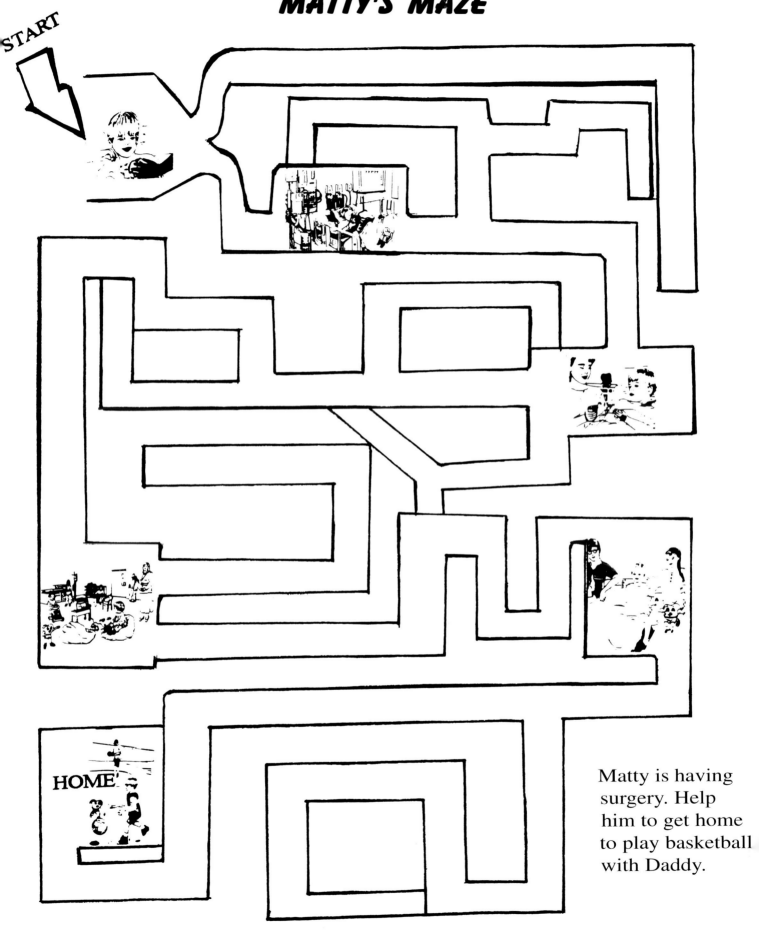

CROSSWORD PUZZLE

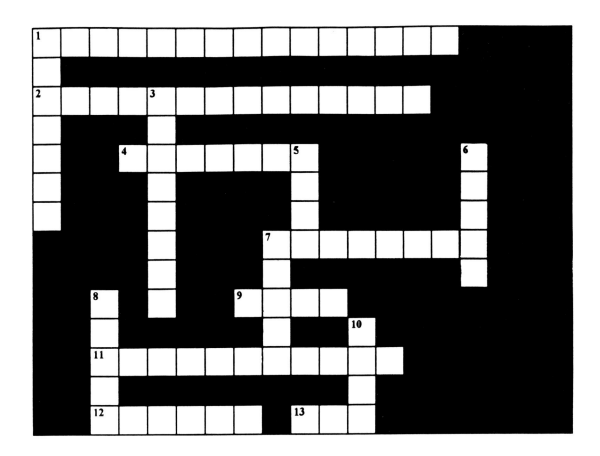

Across
1. Carries unoxygenated blood from the right ventricle to the lungs. (Page 10-11)
2. An ultrasound of the heart. (Page 15)
4. A method of pulling mucus out of the lung. (Page 30)
7. So you will sleep during a heart cath either anesthesia or _____ is given. (Page 18)
9. This is important in the recovery process, just don't baby him. (Page 38)
11. What is the name of the first chamber of the heart that receives unoxygenated blood. (Page 10)
12. This helps keep the lungs cleared out. (Page 38)
13. A graphic representation of the electrical activity of the heart. (Page 13)

Down
1. The cavity of the body, where the blood and fluid collect after surgery. This is where a chest tube is inserted into. (Page 29)
3. It is important to do this after your breathing tube is removed. (Page 34)
5. The SA _____ is where electrical activity is initiated in the heart. (Page 13)
6. A catheter that drains urine out of the bladder. (Page 31)
7. A wire cage placed in an artery to help keep it open. (Page 18)
8. Carries blood from the left ventricle to the body. (Page 10-11)
10. Where your unoxygenated blood becomes oxygenated. (Page 10-11)

WHO AM I?

1. I pump your blood all over your body, who am I? (Page 7)

   _____

2. I give the blood oxygen (air), who am I? (Page 10 - 11)

   _____

3. I am the arch that carries the blood from the heart to the body, who am I? (Page 10 - 11)

   _____

4. I start the electrical activity of the heart, who am I? (Page 13)

   _____

5. I carry blood from the right ventricle to the lungs, who am I? (Page 10 - 11)

   _____

6. I have a right and a left and am the two lower chambers of the heart, who am I? (Page 10 - 11)

   _____

7. I have a right and a left and am the two upper chambers of the heart, who am I? (Page 10 - 11)

   _____

Word Find

```
L E F T V E N T R I C L E B F
S U C T I O N D V P M P K R O
X A V A C A N E V U C I G C L
B L E F T A T R I U M G Y S E
P U L M O N A R Y A R T E R Y
B X R A Y S T E N T B E C S L
L U S B G A G T N E S I S U S
O U H G T N L F H B C D O R F
O U C H P O W E E P S G C E N
D C G P P D T A A O R T A P O
C I P Q R E S T R M A T T Y D
R I G H T V E N T R I C L E E
```

1. AORTA
2. BLOOD
3. EKG
4. FOLEY
5. OWEE
6. REST
7. OUCH
8. STENT
9. LUNG
10. SUCTION
11. SA NODE
12. HEART
13. MATTY
14. XRAY
15. RIGHT VENTRICLE
16. LEFT ATRIUM
17. RIGHT ATRIUM
18. VENA CAVA
19. PULMONARY ARTERY
20. LEFT VENTRICLE

ANSWER PAGE

Solution to the WORD FIND

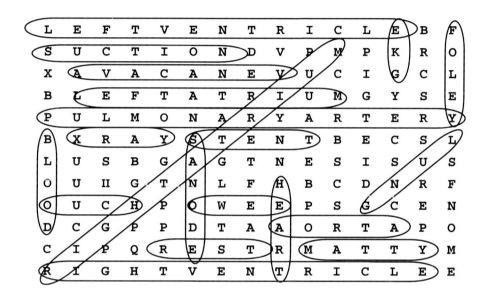

Solution to the CROSSWORD PUZZLE

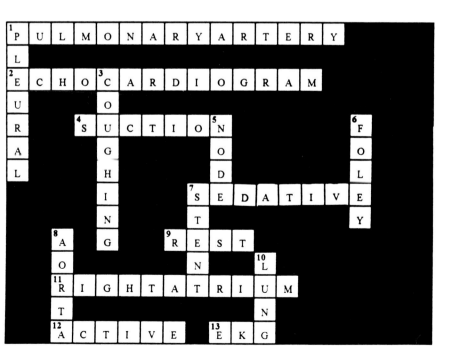

solutions to WHO AM I?

1. Heart
2. Lung
3. Aorta
4. SA Node
5. Pulmonary Artery
6. Ventricles
7. Atrium